The Wonderful World of Nature

ARCTURUS

ARCTURUS

This edition published in 2022
by Arcturus Publishing Limited
26/27 Bickels Yard, 151–153 Bermondsey Street,
London SE1 3HA

Author: Polly Cheeseman
Illustrator: Iris Deppe
Designer: Stefan Holliland
Editor: Violet Peto
Consultant: Anne Rooney
Managing Editor: Joe Harris

ISBN: 978-1-3988-1537-7
CH010038NT
Supplier 29, Date 0722, PI 00001967

Printed in China

Contents

Wonderful Nature

In this book you'll discover amazing animals, brilliant birds, incredible insects, and tremendous trees. There are also fun activities to try and quizzes to test your knowledge. Take a look ...

Explore the ocean and the weird and wonderful creatures that live there.

Find out about animals, from slithering snakes to curious meerkats.

Take to the skies with beautiful birds of all different shapes and sizes.

Get busy with nature activities— plant a seed, or make a bath for your feathered friends.

Wonder at the amazing lives of insects and other creepy-crawlies.

Discover the beauty and strength of trees, and why our planet depends on them.

All About Animals

All the Animals

From the bottom of the oceans to the skies above us, our planet is filled with millions of incredible creatures. We group animals by things that they have in common.

All birds have feathers and wings—though not all birds can fly. Birds lay eggs, which their chicks hatch from. They are warm-blooded, have bony skeletons, and breathe air.

Reptiles, such as snakes, lizards, and turtles, are cold-blooded, which means that they need to warm themselves in the sun. Their skin is tough and scaly. Most reptile babies hatch from eggs.

6

Like birds and reptiles, all **mammals** have bony skeletons and breathe air. Mammals are warm-blooded. This means that their bodies keep their temperature stable whether they are in hot or cold places. Most mammals have hair, and their babies drink their mother's milk.

People are mammals, too!

Amphibians, such as frogs and toads, begin life in water. As adults, most can also live on land. Their skin needs to be kept damp. They breathe with **gills**, lungs, or through their skin.

Invertebrates are creatures that do not have a skeleton inside their bodies. They include flying insects, soft-bodied worms, and sea creatures, such as crabs and sea anemones.

Fish live under water in rivers, lakes, and oceans. Their bodies are covered with scales, and they have fins to help them swim. They use their gills to take in **oxygen** from the water.

On the Hunt

Wolves are famous for their loud howl. Wolves are **predators**, which means they hunt other animals for food.

Wolves live in groups called packs. The pack is made up of a male and female leader, and their young. There can be as many as 30 wolves in a pack.

Wolves hunt in packs. They signal to each other and try and surround their **prey**. By working together, wolves can bring down large animals, such as moose and deer.

Moose

Wolves have large ears and excellent hearing. They can hear prey from far away. They are also able to hear the howls of other wolves.

With long, strong legs, wolves are able to sprint after fast-moving prey. Wolves travel long distances searching for food.

A wolf has powerful jaws and sharp teeth. This helps the wolf grip onto its prey.

Coral Reef

A **coral reef** is like an amazing underwater garden. Found in **tropical** seas, coral reefs provide food and shelter for thousands of bright and beautiful creatures.

Coral is made by a group of tiny creatures called polyps. The polyps build a hard bony home around themselves. Over many years, different corals join to form large reefs.

Groups of brightly-patterned fish dart in and out of the coral, looking for food. The reef is filled with handy places where fish can hide from **predators**.

Moorish idol

Finger coral

Sea slug

Reef sharks hunt for small fish in the warm, shallow waters.

Sea turtles come to the reef to feed on sea creatures such as jellyfish and sea sponges. Like other aquatic **reptiles**, turtles must swim to the surface to breathe air.

Butterfly fish

Sea sponge

Family Life

Elephants are the largest land animal. Even though they are strong and powerful, these **mammals** are gentle giants. Elephants look after their young for longer than any other animal—apart from humans.

Elephants live in family groups. Families can join together to form larger **herds.** The oldest female is the leader. She helps the others find water and watches over them when they rest.

A female elephant carries her baby inside her for nearly two years before it is born. This is longer than any other mammal. A baby elephant is called a calf.

When a calf is born, the mother uses her trunk to help it stand and drink her milk. The calf can walk soon after it's born. The calf stays with its mother for up to 10 years.

Mother

Calf

Other elephants in the herd help look after the young. They protect calves from **predators**. By watching their elders, calves learn to use their trunks to pick grass and leaves to eat.

13

Amazing Amphibians

Frogs, toads, and salamanders all belong to a group of animals called **amphibians**. As adults, most amphibians are able to live on land and in the water.

Amphibians are cold-blooded, which means that they cannot control their body temperature. They become warmer or cooler depending on their surroundings.

Even though most amphibians have lungs to breathe, they take in most of their **oxygen** through their skin. Their smooth skin needs to be kept damp, so they stay close to water.

Salamanders look a bit like lizards. Most are small, but the Chinese giant salamander is the largest in the world. It can grow longer than the height of a man!

Some amphibians have bright or patterned skin. This is a warning for **predators** not to attack them. Their skin can taste nasty and even contain poison!

Frogs have very long and strong back legs. They use them to leap on land and to swim under water. Tree frogs have sticky pads on their feet to help them climb.

Red-eyed tree frog

Sticky pads

Strong back legs

Toads may look like frogs, but usually they are larger and spend more time on land than frogs do. Their skin looks dry and bumpy. Some toads croak very loudly.

15

The Life of a Frog

Most amphibians start life looking very different to how they look as adults. A frog's body goes through big changes as it grows. This is called **metamorphosis**.

First, the female frog lays a big blob of eggs in water. She can lay more than a thousand eggs. The eggs are called frogspawn. Each egg has a jellylike layer around a dark spot.

1

6

When the young frogs are fully grown, they can make babies of their own!

5

The froglets crawl out of the water. They look like tiny frogs with stubby tails. They now have lungs and can breathe air.

Tiny tadpoles hatch from the eggs. They have long tails that they use to swim. They take **oxygen** from the water using **gills**. Tadpoles eat pondweed.

2

3

As the tadpoles grow larger, back legs appear. Their heads become more pointed in shape. Tadpoles start to eat other animals, as well as plants.

4

Next, the front legs form on the tadpoles. At the same time, their tails become shorter. They are now called froglets.

17

Make a Mini Wildlife Pond

Many animals make their homes in or around a pond. Attract tiny creatures to your backyard by making your own mini pond. You'll need a watertight container— the bigger, the better.

Old plastic container

1

Find a good spot for your mini pond—some shade is best. Ask an adult to help you dig a hole to fit your container in.

2

When your container is in place, add a layer of stones and gravel at the bottom. Create different levels with larger rocks.

Pond plants

3 At one side, add logs and rocks to create "steps." This will help creatures get in and out of your pond.

4 Time to fill your pond! Natural rainwater is best for this. Leave some containers out in the rain, so you can use them to fill your mini pond.

5 Planting a few water plants will make your pond more natural and keep the water clear. You can buy these at garden stores.

6 If slimy green algae forms, scoop it out with a stick. It may take a while for creatures to visit your pond. Watch for bugs, dragonflies, and frogs!

Gravel

African Grasslands

The great grasslands of Africa are home to many different animals.

Large **herds** of grass-eating animals roam the land, watched by hungry meat-eating **predators**. There are only two seasons here—a hot, dry season and a rainy season.

Oryx

Hyenas hunt in packs and also gobble up other predators' leftovers.

Lions live in groups called prides. These big cats are **carnivores**, which means that they only eat meat. They hunt zebra, wildebeest, antelope, or any other animal they can catch!

Giraffe

Giraffes are known for their long legs and neck. Their great height means that they can reach the juiciest leaves from the treetops.

Beautiful striped zebras are **herbivores**, meaning that they only eat plants, such as grass. Their stripes make it hard for predators to pick out a single zebra in the herd.

Warthogs are a type of wild pig. They push their snouts in the ground, snuffling up grasses and plant roots. Warthogs are surprisingly fast runners.

Warthog

Gentle Giants

Pandas are a type of bear. These large **mammals** live in chilly mountain forests in China. Giant pandas are very particular about the food they eat. They only eat the stems and leaves of the bamboo plant.

Bamboo is not very **nutritious**, so giant pandas have to eat a LOT of it. They eat for up to 16 hours a day, chomping up to 600 bamboo stems!

Bamboo

Despite their size, giant pandas are excellent tree climbers. They "hug" the tree trunk and use their sharp claws to grip onto the bark.

It can get very cold in the forest. Giant pandas have thick, waterproof fur that keeps them warm and dry during snowy winters.

A baby panda is called a cub. When it's born, the cub is small and pink, and has hardly any hair. It feeds on its mother's milk.

Red pandas are not related to giant pandas, although they both eat bamboo. These long-tailed mammals are about the same size as a cat.

In the Freezer

One of the coldest places on Earth is the freezing Arctic. Despite this, many creatures survive there. Some animals are white, so that they blend in with the ice and snow.

Arctic foxes have thick fur to keep them warm—even under their feet! When they sleep, they wrap their bushy tails around themselves like a blanket.

Walrus

Ringed seal

Walruses and seals have a layer of fat under their skin called blubber. This keeps out the cold when they dive for fish and other sea creatures.

Polar bears are the largest **predators** in the Arctic. They have an excellent sense of smell and can sniff out **prey** from far away. Polar bears hunt seals.

Whales are **marine mammals**. They spend all their lives at sea, but they come to the surface to breathe. Beluga whales are the only white whale. They feed on fish in the chilly Arctic Sea.

Scaly Reptiles

This group of animals has dry, tough skin that is covered in scales. Some reptiles, such as crocodiles and turtles, spend much of their life in the water. However, all reptiles breathe air.

Reptiles are cold-blooded, so they need to "bask," or warm themselves, in the sun. This is why most reptiles live in warm places. If it gets too hot, they find shade to cool down.

Crocodiles and alligators are the largest reptiles, known for their sharp teeth and strong jaws. They use their long, powerful tails to push themselves through lakes and rivers.

Texas tortoise

Unlike turtles, which live in water, tortoises live on land and eat plants. They have a bony shell on their back that protects them. Some tortoises can live to be 100 years old.

Most reptiles lay eggs. When the eggs hatch, reptile babies look like tiny versions of their parents. Many reptile babies have to look after themselves.

A crocodile's eyes and nostrils are on top of its snout. It can see and smell **prey** while its body is hidden below the surface.

Nile crocodile

The most common type of reptile are lizards. Most lizards have long tails and walk on four legs. They eat insects and other small creatures.

Snakes have long bodies and no legs. They can open their jaws very wide and swallow their prey whole. Some snakes are **venomous**, but most are harmless to humans.

Sand lizard

Milk snake

27

Deep-Sea Hunters

There are hundreds of different types of sharks, but the hammerhead may look the strangest! Its eyes are on both sides of its wide, flat head. This helps the hammerhead see to the sides.

Sharks have rows of sharp teeth that grow all the time. When a tooth wears down or falls out, a new tooth moves forward to take its place.

Eye

Sharks have amazing senses. They can detect tiny electric currents in the water. Hammerheads use these currents, along with their great sense of smell, to find food.

Hammerheads live in warm waters near the coast. They sweep their heads from side to side as they swim, scanning the ocean for **prey**.

Squid

Great hammerhead shark

Hammerheads eat sea creatures, such as fish, squid, crabs, and even other sharks! They use their wide heads to pin stingray to the ocean floor.

Stingray

Special Skills

Animals can go to great lengths to find a tasty meal—or to avoid becoming one! While some creatures are able to blend into the background, others can perform clever tricks.

Armadillos mostly eat insects, such as termites. If these shy creatures sense danger, they run to hide in an underground burrow.

The armadillo is an unusual **mammal**. It has tough, scaly skin and hard, bony plates running from the tip of its nose to the end of its tail.

An animal's ability to blend into its surroundings is called camouflage. A tiger's stripes allow it to hide among plants, so it can sneak up on **prey**.

An armadillo's bony plates act like a shield. They protect the armadillo's soft body parts from attack by birds, foxes, and other **predators**.

If an armadillo is attacked, it rolls itself up into a tough, bony ball. This keeps even the most fearsome predator from taking a bite!

Bony plates

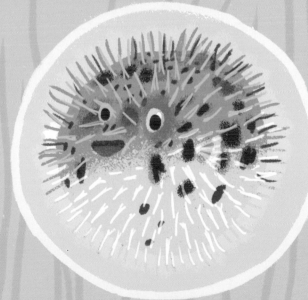

The chameleon's skin changes from green to brown, depending on how it feels. When it's angry, it turns stripy to warn off predators.

The **poisonous** porcupine fish is covered with sharp spines to put off predators. When threatened, it blows up its body like a spiky balloon!

Living Together

Meerkats are mammals known for standing upright on their two back legs. They live in large groups called mobs. Meerkats make their homes in large underground burrows in the deserts and grasslands of southern Africa.

Meerkats take turns to keep lookout while the others find food. If a meerkat spots a **predator**, it squeals a warning call to the rest of the mob.

Meerkats eat insects, **reptiles** and bird eggs, and even snakes and scorpions. When a meerkat eats a scorpion, it bites off the stinging tail first, so it doesn't get hurt.

Scorpion

32

Meerkat babies are called pups. All of the adults look after the pups, not just their parents. When an adult is babysitting, it can go the whole day without eating.

Meerkats depend on each other. When it's chilly, they snuggle together to keep warm. They will clean each other by getting rid of dirt and insects from their fur.

Life in the Desert

How do animals survive the dry heat of the desert? Some creatures burrow into the sand to escape from the burning sun. Others can go for a long time without food or water.

Fennec foxes have very large ears to help get rid of too much body heat. They also use them to hear insects and other small **prey**.

Fennec fox

Saharan silver ants are the world's fastest ants. They mostly stay in nests under the sand. They come out to find food for just 10 minutes a day. Their silvery hairs reflect the Sun's rays.

A camel can go for weeks without much food or water. It stores fat in its hump, which it uses for energy. Long eyelashes help keep the sand out of its eyes.

The **venomous** horned viper snake moves sideways very quickly across the desert. It buries itself in the sand and waits for birds and small **mammals** to wander by.

Jerboa

On the Move

Every year, some animals will go on a long and dangerous journey. They do this to search for fresh food, escape the winter, or to have babies. This journey is called **migration**.

Although they live on land, Christmas Island red crabs must have their babies in the sea. Every year, these crabs travel from their forest homes to the shore.

The red crabs' migration looks spectacular but is very dangerous. The crabs have to cross roads and avoid being eaten by other animals!

Wildebeest live in huge **herds** of around a million animals. They travel hundreds of miles across two African countries, searching for fresh grass and water.

Crabs are **invertebrates**. Instead of a skeleton inside their bodies, they are covered with a tough shell. Crabs keep shedding their shells as they grow.

The males dig burrows, where the females stay. After two weeks, the females leave the burrow and release their eggs into the sea. Then, the crabs walk home again!

Arctic terns have the longest animal migration. To escape from the coldest weather, they fly from the North Pole to the South Pole—and back again!

Big Bouncers

Kangaroos belong to a special group of mammals called **marsupials**. Marsupials keep partly developed babies in a pouch. Standing up to 2m (6ft 6in) tall, kangaroos are the largest marsupials. Most marsupials live in Australia.

A baby marsupial is called a joey. When it's born, the joey is tiny, blind, and hairless. It crawls through the mother's fur to a special pouch on her belly to grow.

Joey

The joey feeds on its mother's milk inside the pouch. A kangaroo joey is carried in the pouch until it's a year old.

Pouch

38

Kangaroos get around by jumping on their powerful back legs. They can leap a distance of nearly 10m (32 ft) in a single bound.

The kangaroo's pouch is also useful for escaping **predators**. If the mother spots danger, the joey hides in the pouch. When the mother bounds away, the joey hitches a ride!

Koalas are another Australian marsupial.

These sleepy creatures spend most of their time snoozing in trees. A koala mother's muscles hold the pouch closed, so the koala joey doesn't fall out as she climbs.

Out in the Dark

When you're fast asleep, lots of creatures explore the quiet streets of towns and cities. Animals that are only active at night are called **nocturnal**. They are adapted to life in the darkness.

Moth

Nocturnal animals use the darkness to hunt or to hide from **predators**. Some might need to stay out of the heat of the day.

Foxes can be seen sniffing around streets at night. They often eat waste food that people have thrown away.

Owls are birds of **prey**. They hunt mice, frogs, and other small creatures. Their large eyes and excellent hearing help them find prey in the dark.

Bats are the only **mammals** that can truly fly. Bats squeak as they fly, and listen for the echoes, which helps them find moths to eat.

Tawny owl

The European hedgehog can roll into a spiky ball to protect itself from nighttime hunters. It feeds on small **invertebrates**, such as slugs, snails, and insects.

Mouse

Collect Animal Footprints

Have you ever wondered which animals live near your home? Make an animal footprint trap, and find out if you have any backyard visitors!

1 Use an old baking sheet or tray for your footprint trap. Fill it with damp sand and pat to make a smooth surface. Check that your finger leaves a mark in the sand.

Fine sand

2 Put a little meaty pet food in a shallow dish or an old jar lid. Place the dish in the middle of your footprint trap.

PET FOOD

Fox

Cat

Rabbit

Find a quiet spot outside, and place the footprint trap carefully on the ground. Leave it overnight.

4

Next morning, check for footprints in the sand. Use the guide at the bottom of the page to help you find out which creatures visited!

Sunflower seeds

Rather than pet food, try putting out seeds, lettuce leaves, and chopped unsalted nuts. Do you get different footprints?

Bird

Squirrel

Mouse

Venom and Poison

Not all animals are cute and cuddly! **Venomous** animals inject harmful substances into their enemies by biting or stinging them. Other creatures are **poisonous**, which means that they will harm animals that eat or touch them.

Scorpions are **invertebrates**. They have eight legs and two large pincers, which they use to tear up **prey**. Their long tails are tipped with a venomous sting.

Scorpions can sense tiny movements on the ground or in the air. They lie still and wait for prey to come close—then they attack!

Deathstalker scorpion

The box jellyfish has long tentacles covered with stinging cells. It uses its deadly venom to catch its prey. A box jellyfish can even kill a human.

Sting

The deathstalker is thought to be one of the world's deadliest scorpions. It uses its venomous sting to kill prey and to protect itself from **predators**.

Deathstalker scorpions usually eat insects, worms, and other scorpions. These desert-dwelling creatures can live for up to a year on just one meal!

Many amphibians are poisonous if they are eaten. The most poisonous is the golden poison dart frog. Just one of these tiny frogs could kill 10 people.

When they are threatened, spitting cobras can spray venom out of their fangs. The cobra's venom is powerful enough to blind its victim.

45

Friendly Dolphins

Dolphins spend all their lives in the sea. Like all marine mammals, they must swim to the surface to breathe air. With their sleek bodies and powerful tails, dolphins are superfast swimmers.

Bottlenose dolphin

Dolphins live in groups called pods. The dolphins play together and look after each other. They work as a team to hunt fish and other sea creatures.

Dolphins call to each other with clicks and squeaks. Each dolphin makes its own special sound. If a dolphin calls for help, the rest of the pod will swim to find it.

Blowhole

A dolphin breathes through its "blowhole," which is a hole on the top of its head. When a dolphin surfaces, it sprays water out of its blowhole.

When a dolphin sleeps, half of its brain always stays awake. Because they have to swim up for air, dolphins cannot sleep deeply.

Animals in Danger

Some animals are endangered. This means that there are not many of them left in the wild.

Animals usually become endangered because of things that people do, such as hunting them or damaging their **habitats**.

Orangutan means "man of the forest." Orangutans belong to a group of **mammals** called great apes, which includes gorillas, chimpanzees—and us!

There are seven types of sea turtles, and all are in danger. Some turtles mistake plastic bags floating in the water for jellyfish and eat them.

Rhinoceroses are large **herbivores**. They live in Asia and Africa and are hunted for their horns. However, people are working hard to protect them.

Orangutans live in **rain forest**s in Asia. They use their long arms to swing through the trees, looking for fruit to eat.

Because their forest homes are being cleared for farming, the number of orangutans has become smaller. However, lots of people are working to help orangutans.

Wildlife reserves have been set up to protect orangutans and other animals. Wildlife reserves are huge areas of land where hunting and the cutting down of trees are not allowed.

Years ago, people hunted humpback whales, and they nearly died out completely. Thankfully, since whale hunting was banned, the number of humpback whales has gone up. They are no longer endangered!

Animals Quiz

Put your knowledge about animals to the test. Decide if these sentences are true or false, then check your answers on page 191. No peeping!

1 Elephants live their whole lives alone.

2 The female frog lays her eggs in water.

3 The most common type of reptile are lizards.

4 Porcupine fish are harmless.

5 Bats are the only mammals that can truly fly.

6 Dolphins are land mammals.

50

All About Birds

Beautiful Birds

From the frozen ice sheets of Antarctica, to the dry deserts of Africa, birds live all over the world. They come in lots of different shapes and sizes, but all birds have some things in common.

Birds are the only animals that have feathers. Feathers keep birds warm, dry, and help them fly. Birds keep their feathers clean with their beaks.

Flight feathers

Eurasian jay

52

All birds hatch from eggs. The chicks grow inside the eggs. Bird parents sit on their eggs to keep them warm until they are ready to hatch.

Instead of teeth, birds have beaks. A bird's beak is perfectly shaped for the type of food it eats. This jay uses its strong bill to crack open acorns.

All birds have wings, but not all birds can fly. Flying birds have strong chest muscles, which help them beat their wings.

Expert Hunters

The group of birds that hunt for their food and attack with their claws are called **birds of prey**. Among the largest and most powerful birds of prey are eagles.

Bald eagle

Eagles have amazing eyesight that is more than twice as sharp as a human's. Eagles can spot their **prey** from high up in the sky.

The Andean condor is the largest and heaviest bird of prey. It has a wingspan of 3 m (10 ft). These birds feed on the bodies of dead animals, such as deer and cows.

Its huge wings let the eagle glide easily through the air. It soars high up to get a good view of animals below, then swoops down to attack.

Eagles have very strong, sharp claws called **talons**. Bald eagles use their talons to catch fish, grasping them tightly until they reach their nests.

Birds of prey have powerful beaks that are hooked and very sharp.

The peregrine falcon is the world's fastest-flying bird. When it spots prey, it pulls in its wings and dives down to attack at speeds of more than 250 kph (155 mph).

Nest Building

Most birds build nests. These are safe places, where eggs and chicks can be protected from **predators**. Nests can be made from lots of different materials, including twigs, moss, mud, and spiderwebs.

Tailorbirds live in Asia. They get their name from the way they build their nests. They "sew" leaves using their beaks, like a tailor sews cloth.

The male tailorbird gathers the materials and keeps watch.

Ovenbirds collect mud and place it on a tree branch. Bit by bit, more mud is added to form a rounded shape. The mud nest bakes hard in the sun.

To make their nests, woodpeckers carve a hole in a tree using their strong beaks. When the hole is ready, they lay their eggs inside.

56

First, a female tailorbird finds a strong leaf, which is still attached to the tree. She makes tiny holes along the leaf using her needle-sharp beak.

The female uses tiny strands of plants and spiderwebs to stitch the leaf into a cup shape.

Spiderweb thread

The male tailorbird helps fill the leaf with soft pieces of plants, animal fur, and feathers. The nest is made so carefully that the leaf stays green and alive!

Woodpecker

Being waterbirds, swans need to build their large nests close to the water's edge. The nest is a huge mound of grasses, rushes, and other plants.

57

Bringing up Blue Tits

Every spring, adult blue tits prepare to raise a family. They look for holes in trees, walls, or use human-made birdhouses. Discover how these pretty birds hatch and grow during their first weeks of life.

The female makes a cup-shaped nest in a nesting hole using moss, grass, and leaves. She lines it with soft feathers and animal hair.

The blue tit lays one egg a day. She lays around 10 eggs altogether. While she sits on the eggs to keep them warm, her partner brings her food.

After two weeks, the eggs are ready to hatch. Blue tit chicks are blind, featherless, and helpless when they hatch. The mother sits on them to keep them warm.

Both parents feed the chicks with hundreds of fresh caterpillars throughout the day. The chicks' mouths are bright yellow— easy for the parents to see.

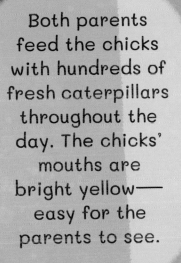

The chicks grow quickly. After just a few weeks, they can begin flying. The chick is now called a **fledgling**. Chicks leave the nest a few weeks later.

City Birds

Many different birds have adapted to life in towns and cities. Birds make their calls louder to be heard over the traffic noise. They also depend on people for some of their food.

Blue jay

Pretty house finches like to visit people's backyards. As well as gobbling up insects, finches love to eat sunflower seeds from bird feeders.

American robin

European starling

60

American crows are not fussy about their food— they eat pretty much anything they can find! They gather in large groups to **roost** at night.

House sparrows hop around busy areas, looking for crumbs to peck. Some sparrows are so friendly, they will even eat from your hand!

Northern cardinal

Pigeons are a common sight on city streets. They can be seen perching on buildings and under bridges. They often eat food that people have dropped.

61

Make a Bird Feeder

Want to attract birdlife to your backyard? Get busy in the kitchen and make this tasty treat. Then sit back and wait for your feathered friends!

Ask a grown-up to help you make a hole through the middle of an apple using a skewer or apple corer.

1

Push some string through the hole in the apple. Tie the string around a thin stick or chopstick, so that the apple sits on top.

2

3

Carefully push seeds into the apple skin, until the apple is covered. Sunflower seeds work well for this—and birds love them!

European robin

Chaffinch

Blackbird

4 Use the other end of the string to hang up your apple bird feeder outside. Choose a place where you can watch the birds without disturbing them.

How many different types of birds visit your feeder?

Brilliant Beaks

The shape of a bird's beak, or bill, helps it eat the type of food it likes. Toucans are well known for their huge beaks, which they use to eat fruit.

Toucans live in **rain forest** trees in South America. They use their long bills to reach fruits growing high up in the forest **canopy**.

Toco toucan

The northern shoveler is a "dabbling" duck, which means that it feeds at the water's surface. Its wide, flat bill acts like a sieve, filtering insects and plants to eat.

Finches, such as the Atlantic canary, have cone-shaped beaks. This shape makes the beak powerful enough to crack open the hard seeds that finches love.

The toucan's bill is very long compared to its body. The bill is around one-third of the bird's total body length!

The edges of the toucan's beak are jagged, or "serrated." This means that it can get a firm grip on its meal.

The beak is hollow, which makes it lightweight despite its size. The toucan's tongue is long and shaped a little bit like a feather.

Atlantic canary

The long, curved bill of the curlew is perfect for digging up food from mud. This wading bird uses its beak like tweezers to pluck out tiny creatures.

Emperor Penguin

The emperor penguin cannot fly, but it is an expert swimmer! These large birds are perfectly adapted to life in Antarctica—the coldest place on Earth.

Emperor penguins have a thick layer of fat under their skin. This keeps them warm. Their feathers are packed tightly together to keep out the freezing wind.

Emperor penguin chicks are covered with fluffy feathers. The parents keep their chick snug by balancing it on their feet, away from the icy ground.

Chick

Emperor penguins live in large groups called colonies. The **colony** huddles together for warmth. Each penguin takes its turn standing on the outside, where it's coldest.

Penguins use their small wings as flippers to power through the water. They can dive for nearly half an hour, hunting fish and other sea creatures.

Down by the River

Many different birds make their homes in and around rivers and streams. Waterbirds spend much of their time swimming and feeding. Other birds watch for fish from the riverbank.

Mallard

Common kingfisher

Ducks, such as mallards, have webbed feet, which are perfect for paddling through the water. They dip their heads under the surface to feed on water plants.

The bright and beautiful kingfisher will wait patiently on a branch for its next meal to swim by. It nests in a burrow on the riverbank.

Herons keep perfectly still for a long time. When they spot a tasty-looking fish, they plunge their long, stabbing beaks into the water.

Swans are large waterbirds that weigh around the same a as 7-year-old child. They use their long necks to reach for plants under the water.

Fantastic Fliers

Being able to fly allows birds to escape enemies, find food, or travel to warmer places. Different birds fly in different ways, depending on the size and shape of their wings.

Pigeons and doves fly by flapping their pointed wings continuously, so they have strong chest muscles to power them. They can fly at speeds of 80 kph (50 mph).

The tail helps the bird steer. It is also used for balance when the bird perches on a branch or walks on the ground.

The wandering albatross is the largest seabird in the world. It spends most of its life at sea, gliding for great distances with its long, narrow wings.

Eurasian collared dove

The largest and strongest feathers are the flight feathers. The different parts of each feather link together to make a flat surface.

A bird's skeleton needs to be tough, but lightweight, in order to fly. Flying birds have hollow bones with special struts inside to make them superstrong.

Flight feathers

Many small birds, such as the chickadee, have rounded wings. Chickadees fly by flapping their wings quickly, then gliding in order to save energy.

Fabulous Flamingos

With their huge beaks, long legs, and bright pink feathers, flamingos are amazing-looking birds. They live in large colonies on the edges of lakes, or near shallow areas of water.

Flamingos are very noisy. Although there can be thousands of flamingos in a **colony**, a parent can find its chick by listening for its own special call.

Flamingos eat **plankton**, which is made up of tiny plants and animals. The plankton contains chemicals that turn flamingo feathers pink or red.

Flamingos are often seen standing on one leg, but it isn't known why. When looking for a **mate**, a group of flamingos will perform a kind of dance together!

When a flamingo feeds, it turns its head upside down and puts its beak under the water. The beak has bristles inside, which trap the plankton.

73

Nighttime Birds

Just like us, most birds are active during the day.

Owls have super senses. Their large eyes see extremely well in dim light. They also have excellent hearing and can hear tiny creatures from far away.

But when the sun goes down, some birds are getting ready for the night ahead. Owls are the best-known nocturnal birds.

Nightjars are nocturnal birds with mottled, brown feathers. As they fly, they open their beaks wide to catch nighttime insects, such as moths.

Unlike other birds, owls have large, forward-facing eyes. This means it can spot movement and judge distance from high above its **prey**.

The edges of an owl's flight feathers are fringed and soft. This allows the owl to fly very quietly, so its prey doesn't hear it coming.

The great horned owl is the largest owl in North America. It is a fierce **predator** and sometimes hunts other owls.

The kiwi is a fluffy-looking **flightless bird** from New Zealand. It walks about at night, sniffing out worms, insects, and fallen fruit to eat.

During the day, the black-crowned night heron **roosts** in trees close to wetlands. At sunset, it comes out to feed on fish and other creatures.

75

Along the Coast

Lots of birds can be seen by the seashore, because there is plenty of food here. Some birds catch fish at sea, while others wait on the beach to see what's been washed up.

Cormorants nest in cliffs along the coastline. They are excellent swimmers and will dive under the water to catch fish with their hooked beaks.

Fluttering among the rocks, the turnstone flips stones looking for food underneath. It can turn over rocks the same size as its body!

Gulls are a common sight and sound on the coast. Herring gulls don't just eat herrings. They will eat almost anything they can find!

Oystercatchers are wading birds. They walk along the shoreline, using their long beaks to crack open shellfish, such as cockles and mussels.

Ringed plover

Incredible Divers

Some birds are as skilled in the water as they are in the air. Diving birds, such as pelicans, plunge into the ocean, hunting for fish to eat.

Brown pelican

Pelicans are large diving birds with huge beak pouches, which they use to scoop up fish. Their pouches can hold three times more water than their stomachs can!

The brown pelican hunts by flying over the surface of the ocean and diving in head first. It takes in large gulps of water and fish.

The pelican pushes the water out of its bill with its throat muscles. Then, it swallows the fish left inside its beak.

The Atlantic puffin dives from the water's surface, using its wings like flippers. Its bright bill has jagged edges, allowing it to hold up to 60 small fish at once!

As well as being expert divers, pelicans can glide long distances using their extremely large wings. Their wingspan is greater than the height of a man.

Pretty Parrots

With their bright feathers and noisy squawks, parrots are very clever and friendly birds. Macaws are a type of parrot that lives in warm, **tropical rain forests** in South America.

Blue and gold macaw

Macaws are large, fast-flying parrots with long tails. They live high up in tall rain forest trees. Macaws stay with the same partner for life.

The cockatoo uses its striking head **crest** to let others know how it's feeling. It raises its crest if it is excited or surprised.

Cockatiels are small and slim members of the cockatoo family. They live in Australia and make their nests in tree holes.

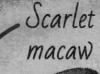
Scarlet
macaw

There are lots of
different kinds of
macaws, each with
their own markings.
The scarlet macaw
has a red head and
body, and bright blue
and yellow wings.

Macaws eat fruit,
nuts, and seeds. Their
powerful bills crack
open seeds and rip
fruit apart. Their
tongues contain a
bone, helping them
open nuts.

Macaws often feed
together in large, noisy
groups. Sometimes, they
gather on clay cliffs
to nibble and lick the
mineral-rich clay.

Clay cliff

Lovebirds are small
parrots that live in dry
areas of Africa. They
are called lovebirds
because of the close
bond a pair of these
birds makes.

Patterns in the Sky

As the sun goes down, thousands of starlings take to the skies and perform amazing flying displays. They fly together in a huge, swooping, moving shape called a **murmuration**.

At first glance, European starlings look like somewhat plain birds. Close up, you'll see their beautiful, glossy feathers with a green and purple sheen.

Winter is a good time to see a
starling murmuration. This is when
starling **flocks** are at their largest
and their displays are the most
spectacular.

Birds gather in large
flocks for safety. It is
harder for **predators**,
such as peregrine falcons,
to pick out one starling in
a huge group.

Starlings
murmurate just
before they **roost**
for the night. They roost
close together in sheltered
places, such as under buildings
and cliffs, keeping each
other warm.

Running Free

Not all birds can fly. To escape danger, some flightless birds have become super-speedy sprinters.

Male ostrich

Female ostrich

The largest and fastest of all flightless birds is the ostrich, which lives on grasslands in Africa.

Chicks

The ostrich is the world's largest bird. It can grow much taller than a man and weigh twice as much. Its huge eyes are bigger than its brain!

Emus are Australia's largest bird. Like their ostrich cousins, they can live in groups. They have long, shaggy tail feathers, which they shake to warn off predators.

Long, strong legs enable the ostrich to run at speeds of 70 kph (43 mph) to escape predators. Its kick is powerful enough to kill a lion.

The ostrich has long, fluffy wing feathers that help it change direction when running fast. An ostrich parent uses its wings to shade its chicks from the sun.

Given its size, it's not surprising that the ostrich lays the world's largest egg. Each egg weighs 30 times more than a chicken egg!

The cassowary sports a bright blue face and neck, and a horny head **crest**. It also has extremely long, knife-like claws, which it uses to defend itself.

Hummingbirds

Beating their wings faster than you can see, these tiny birds have incredible flying skills. Hummingbirds are only found in North and South America, and most types live in **tropical** forests.

Hummingbirds have long, slim bills and even longer tongues. They hover by flowers, pushing their beaks deep inside to drink the **nectar**. They also eat insects.

With their bright, shimmering feathers, hummingbirds look like jewels in the sky. Emerald hummingbirds are named for their sparkling green feathers.

Hummingbird feathers make reflect light, creating a shiny, rainbow effect called "iridescence." Males show off their glittering feathers to attract a **mate**.

Western emerald hummingbird

Hummingbirds can
beat their wings
80 times a second,
which makes a
humming sound. These
birds can hover, fly
backward, and even
fly upside down!

There are around
300 different kinds of
hummingbird. At just
5 cm (2 in) long, the
bee hummingbird is the
smallest bird in the world.

Make a Birdbath

Birds need water to drink and to bathe in. It's important for birds to keep their feathers clean. Taking a dip loosens dirt and makes their feathers easier to look after.

Find a good spot to build your birdbath. An open area is best, so birds have a good view all around them.

Stack up some bricks, or upturned flowerpots, so that your birdbath is off the ground. Make sure you have a stable base.

Bricks

Stones

Place a large shallow dish or circular plant tray on top of the base. Make sure it is heavy enough to be stable. If there is any danger of your birdbath being blown over, ask an adult to strengthen it with superglue.

Flowerpots

Why not decorate your birdbath?

Fill your birdbath with water. Add stones and gravel to make sure it's not too slippery for your feathered friends!

Flying South

Every year, many birds make a very long journey. Birds fly great distances from their summer homes to where they spend the winter. The journey they make is called a **migration**.

Snow geese spend the summer nesting in the Arctic tundra. When it gets colder, the geese fly 1,250 km (2,000 mi) to the Western United States and Mexico.

The geese fly in a V-shape. Each goose follows the bird in front, so they all fly in the same direction. They are careful not to fly into each other.

Snow geese like company when they travel. There can be tens of thousands of snow geese in a **flock**. They can be very noisy!

Along the way, the geese make stops to rest and feed. Some birds will act as lookouts for the flock, watching for predators, such as eagles.

Birds of Paradise

Some creatures go to great lengths in order to find a **mate**. The birds of paradise are a group of birds with beautiful feathers, unusual calls, and very interesting dance moves!

Birds of paradise live in **tropical rain forests** on islands in the Pacific Ocean. There are many kinds, each with their own amazing feathers and displays.

Female birds of paradise are much plainer than the males. Females make sure that they choose the male with the most beautiful feathers.

Female

Males spend a lot of time preparing their display areas. They clear away sticks and prune leaves, so that females get a clear view of them.

The Goldie's bird of paradise puffs up long, fluffy feathers on his back and flaps his wings. He hops about, calling loudly to attract a female.

Goldie's bird of paradise

When he displays, the male superb bird of paradise flicks up his feathers into a cloak-like fan. Bright blue chest and head feathers make him look like a strange smiley face!

From this ...

... to this!

93

Birds Under Threat

Sadly, some birds are in danger. Forest homes are being cut down. Beautiful birds are captured for people to keep as pets. Others are harmed by chemicals.

California condors are **birds of prey** with wingspans of around 3 m (10 ft). Instead of hunting **prey**, they eat animals that are already dead.

The African grey, or African gray, is a beautiful parrot with an amazing ability to copy human voices. Many are stolen from their forest homes to become pets.

The kakapo is a large flightless parrot from New Zealand. It has been hunted by animals, such as cats and rats, which were introduced by people.

Condors have been killed by chemicals that have polluted their **habitat**. Others die because they eat animals that contain harmful substances.

In 1987, there were just 27 California condors left. To keep them from dying out, the last condors were captured and protected in zoos.

A few years later, some California condors were released back into the wild. There are now thought to be around 300 of these magnificent birds.

Kakapo

Kirtland's warblers were once in danger of dying out. Thankfully, their pine forest homes in North America have been protected. Now they are no longer **endangered**!

Birds Quiz

Put your knowledge about birds to the test. Decide if these sentences are true or false, then check your answers on page 191. No peeping!

1 Andean condors only eat insects.

2 Tailorbirds build their nests with mud.

3 Emperor penguins can dive under water for nearly half an hour.

4 Herring gulls only eat herrings.

5 Ostriches lay the largest eggs in the world.

6 Hummingbirds can fly upside down.

All About Insects

Creepy-Crawlies

Most animals on Earth are **invertebrates**, that is, animals without a backbone or skeleton inside their bodies. Take a look around you—there are all kinds of invertebrates everywhere!

Wasp

Arthropods are invertebrates that have a tough outer layer to their bodies instead of a skeleton. This is called an **exoskeleton**. There are different types of arthropods.

Crustaceans are arthropods with 10 or more legs. Many crustaceans, such as lobsters and crabs, live in water. But wood lice are crustaceans, too!

Beetle

Wood lice

Most of the creatures that people call creepy-crawlies, such as bees, beetles, and butterflies, are **insects**. They usually have wings, six jointed legs, and three parts to their bodies.

Arachnids are also arthropods. Most arachnids have eight jointed legs and two body sections. Spiders, scorpions, and mites are all arachnids.

Garden spider

There are a huge number of other kinds of invertebrates. Many soft-bodied invertebrates live under water, but snails, slugs, and worms slither around on land.

Incredible Insects

How would you like to walk upside down on the ceiling, or have eyes as big as your head? **Insects** come in many shapes and sizes, and even the common housefly has amazing abilities.

Insects have **compound eyes**, which are made up of thousands of tiny parts. Compound eyes let insects spot quick movements around them.

A housefly's huge compound eyes cover most of its head. They give the fly a very wide view. It can even see behind itself!

Compound eye

Head

Thorax

Antenna

Abdomen

An insect's body has three parts—the head, **thorax**, and **abdomen**. The two feelers on its head, called **antennae**, are used to smell, touch, or taste.

Most insects have wings. Flies can beat their wings hundreds of times a second. They can fly forward, backward, hover, and flip over to land upside down!

Beautiful Beetles

With around 40,000 different types, beetles form the largest group of **insects**. Beetles live all over the world, in scorching hot and freezing cold places. They can also be found in the park or your own backyard!

Most beetles have two pairs of wings and can fly. The front wing cases are tough and fold over the delicate back wings.

Flying wings

In order to fly, the beetle's wing cases move apart and its long flying wings unfold. Beetles can look a little clumsy when they fly!

Although they look pretty, some kinds of leaf beetles can damage plants. The striped cucumber beetle is seen as a pest because it destroys farmers' crops.

Wing case

Known as ladybirds, ladybugs, or lady beetles, these red, spotted beetles often visit backyards. Gardeners love them, because they eat aphids that destroy plants.

Some beetles' wing cases are bright and patterned. This acts as a warning to other creatures that the beetle is **poisonous**, or tastes bad.

Aphids

Weevils are a type of beetle with a long snout. The beautiful Schoenherr's blue weevil lives on the island of New Guinea, in the Pacific Ocean.

103

Watery World

Many different creatures visit ponds and lakes to find food and lay their eggs. Some **insects** spend the first part of their lives in water, before coming to the surface to breathe air as adults.

Dragonflies dart over the water's surface.

Backswimmers swim on their backs, using their long legs to "row" themselves near the surface. They hold a bubble of air under their wings, so they can breathe under water.

Rams-horn snails live in fresh water, but they need to come to the surface to breathe air. They breathe through their skin.

Red-winged blackbird

Roseate skimmer dragonfly

Whirligig beetles
swim in circles on the surface.
These beetles have two pairs
of eyes—one pair looks
up, and the other pair
looks down under water.

Young dragonflies, called **nymphs**,
live under water. When they're fully
grown, they climb out and change
into adult dragonflies.

Dragonfly
nymph

105

Butterfly Life Cycle

Butterflies go through four different stages in their lives. At the end of each stage, they completely change the way they look and act.
The full sequence of an animal's life is called a **life cycle**.

1

Butterflies lay their eggs on leaves.

Egg

4

Spicebush swallowtail

Inside the cocoon, the caterpillar changes into a butterfly!

This incredible change is called **metamorphosis**.

The eggs hatch into little caterpillars that munch on leaves all day.

2

Cocoon

3

When it is time for a caterpillar to turn into an adult, it makes a cocoon around itself and gets ready to transform.

Make a Butterfly Feeder

Butterflies feed on liquids. They suck up **nectar** from flowers using a curled mouthpart called a **proboscis**. Bring butterflies fluttering to your backyard with this sweet feeder.

1

Use the lid of a large food container or a paper plate for your feeder. Decorate it with a few bright flower shapes using felt-tip pens or paint.

2

Ask an adult to make four equally-spaced holes close to the rim of your feeder. A hole punch is ideal for this.

3

Thread string through the hole and knot to secure. Repeat with the other holes. Gather the four loose ends of string and knot together.

Put chopped fruit onto each flower on your feeder. Use whatever soft fruit you have—the riper, the better.

4

Hang your feeder outside by its string ... and wait!

Red admiral

Holly blue

Tortoiseshell

Do the butterflies prefer a particular fruit?

Try making some sweet liquid by mixing sugar with water. Fill the lid of a jar or bottle with the sugar-water and place on your feeder.

Praying Mantis

It may look like a leaf, but this **insect** is actually a fearsome **predator**. The mantis has two long front legs, which it holds in front of itself as if in prayer.

The praying mantis can turn its head all the way around to look behind it and all around. Its huge eyes spot the slightest movement.

The mantis keeps very still. When an insect comes close, it strikes suddenly with lightning speed. The two front legs shoot out and grab the **prey**.

Many are green to help them hide in leafy surroundings. Some mantises are brown, so that they look like dead leaves, or pink so they look like flowers.

Common praying mantis

The front legs have spines and hooks to grip struggling prey. The mantis starts eating its victim immediately.

Under Attack

Insects and other creepy-crawlies make a tasty meal for lots of different animals. Some bugs warn **predators** with the way they look. Others have clever ways to defend themselves.

Bombardier beetles can be found all over the world. These small beetles live on the ground, among fallen leaves and under stones.

When attacked, a bombardier beetle mixes two chemicals together inside its body. Then, a boiling liquid shoots out of its **abdomen** with a loud "pop."

Ant

The bombardier beetle's liquid weapon is **poisonous**, as well as scalding hot. It is powerful enough to blind or kill a would-be attacker. Luckily, it does not kill humans.

Bees and wasps can give a nasty sting to any creature that bothers them. At first glance, a hoverfly looks like a bee or wasp, so animals keep away.

Hoverfly

Wasp

Bombardier beetle

The bombardier beetle can even direct its spray and aim at a predator. The beetle can fire 20 times before it runs out of liquid.

Stink bugs get their name from the strong smell they make if they are attacked. The man-faced stink bug has markings that warn predators they taste bad, too.

Fuzzy caterpillars can look pretty or cute, but beware. The saddleback caterpillar has stinging spines on its body that inject a painful venom.

113

Making Honey

While some types of bees live on their own, honeybees live in groups called **colonies**. There can be many thousands of bees in a colony, and each has its own role to play.

The "queen" is the mother of all the bees in the nest and is the largest. Her job is laying eggs.

The nest is made up of honeycomb. The honeycomb contains hexagonal "cells."

Larva

Most bees are female "workers." Their job is looking after the hive, the **larvae** (baby bees), and the queen. There are a few males called drones.

Egg

114

Nest

Workers suck up
nectar from flowers,
which turns into honey
inside them. They spit
the honey into the
cells. The honey feeds
the colony.

A larva is the wormlike form that
hatches from an egg. The workers
feed it, and when it is big enough,
they seal it inside the cell.
The larva slowly changes into a bee.
It is called a **pupa** at this stage.
Finally, it breaks out of its cell as an
adult bee.

115

Hairy Hunters

Spiders can be teeny-tiny or huge and hairy!
The largest spiders in the world are tarantulas.
Most tarantulas live in warm forests, where they
hunt **insects**, frogs, and other small creatures.

A tarantula's body is covered
with hairs that sense movements
in the air. Tiny hairs and claws
on the bottom of its feet help the
tarantula run and climb.

With eight long legs,
spiders can run very
fast. Tarantulas often
hide in their underground
burrows. When **prey**
comes near, they leap
out to attack.

Tarantulas use their two fangs to
inject prey with venom. The venom
keeps the prey from moving and
turns its insides into liquid, which
the spider sucks up.

Mexican red-kneed tarantula

Unlike many other spiders, tarantulas do not spin webs. Many tarantulas use their silk to line their burrows. They pull the silk from their bodies using their back legs.

117

Glow in the Dark

Many creepy-crawlies come out at night to avoid being seen, but fireflies do the opposite! These glowing **insects** put on an amazing light show that can be seen for miles.

Also known as lightning bugs, fireflies are not flies or bugs, but beetles. There are more than a thousand different types of fireflies.

To make light, the firefly mixes chemicals in a special organ in its **abdomen**. An animal that can make its own light is said to be bioluminescent.

Fireflies glow to attract a **mate**. Different types of fireflies make their own special light shows. Some flash on and off in a pattern, while others keep glowing.

A firefly's light may also act as a warning signal to **predators**. If eaten, a firefly has a bitter taste and can make some animals sick.

Male European glowworms look like ordinary beetles. At night, the flightless females climb up plant stems and start to glow, in order to attract a mate.

Bugs in Hiding

Some creatures can blend in with their surroundings to help them hide from **predators**— or **prey**. A relative of the walking stick, or stick insect, the leaf insect is one of the best camouflaged animals of all!

It's really hard to spot a leaf insect because it looks almost exactly like a leaf! It can hide in plain sight of predators, such as birds and reptiles.

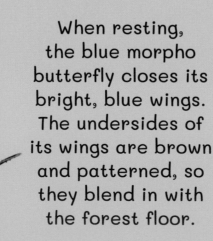

When resting, the blue morpho butterfly closes its bright, blue wings. The undersides of its wings are brown and patterned, so they blend in with the forest floor.

The crab spider perfectly matches the flower it hides in. It waits for **insects** to visit the flower, then attacks.

Leaf insects live in forests, eating the leaves of the plants they live on. Sometimes, leaf insects accidentally take a bite out of each other!

Some leaf insects have brown markings that make them even more realistic. Others are completely brown and look like dead leaves.

Leaf

Leaf insect

Leaf insects usually stay still to avoid being spotted. When they do walk, they sway their bodies and look like real leaves blowing in the breeze.

Sometimes called a jumping stick, the stick grasshopper has a long, twiglike body and legs. It is perfectly camouflaged—until it jumps!

121

Teamwork

Like honeybees, ants live in **colonies**, and each member does a certain job. An ant colony can contain millions of ants. All the ants work together to keep the colony going.

Worker ant

Soldier ant

Larva

Most ants live in nests made from soil, leaves, wood, or sand. Army ants are different—most of the time they are on the move.

Army ants are blind, so they use their long **antennae** to find their way. The ants feed on any creature they come across, attacking with their powerful jaws.

As they travel, workers carry the eggs and **larvae**. Larger "soldier" ants protect them. If there's a gap to pass, army ants form a "bridge" with their bodies.

The queen lays all the eggs in the colony. Workers feed and protect the queen and her larvae. With no fixed nest, the ants make their own temporary shelter. Many ants hold onto each other, making a ball protecting those inside!

Dung Beetles

Dung beetles depend on the droppings of larger animals. They roll animal poop, live in it, lay their eggs in it, and eat it! There are thousands of different kinds of dung beetles living all over the world.

Dung beetles have an excellent sense of smell, sniffing out animal poop from great distances! The dung contains all the water and **nutrients** the beetle needs.

When a beetle finds dung, it rolls it into a ball larger than itself. Then, it rolls the dung ball away using its strong back legs.

For its size, a dung beetle is one of the strongest creatures on Earth. It can move a dung ball that is hundreds of times its own body weight!

Some beetles burrow into the dung ball, eating it from the inside. Females lay their eggs in the middle. When they hatch, the **larvae** eat the dung around them.

By recycling animal poop, dung beetles do an important job. They are natural cleaners, keeping animal dung from piling up and keeping flies at bay!

Dung beetles belong to the family of beetles called scarabs, which were held in high praise by the ancient Egyptians. There are many thousands of types of scarab beetles, and some are very beautiful.

125

On the Forest Floor

Next time you go for a walk in the woods, don't forget to look down. There are many small creatures that make their homes among the fallen leaves and dead wood.

Stag beetles scuttle over logs and stumps, feeding on tree sap. Male stag beetles use their antler-like jaws to attract females and fight enemies.

European stag beetle

Chicken of the woods fungus

Lift up a log, and you'll probably find wood lice underneath. These little **crustaceans** eat rotting wood and plants. They like damp, dark places.

Silver-washed fritillary

Earwigs are found in leaf litter and under bark. They have long pincers on the end of their **abdomens**, which they use to defend themselves.

Moss

Centipedes are **arthropods**. They spend the day hiding in soil or under dead wood. At night, they use their **venomous** fangs to catch insects, worms, and spiders.

Amazing Journey

Every year, millions of monarch butterflies fly up to 4,800 km (3,000 mi) from Canada to Mexico. This incredible journey is called a **migration**. No other butterfly travels as far.

The journey south takes around two months. Monarchs save energy by gliding on air currents. They stop on the way, to rest and drink **nectar**.

Monarchs must avoid being eaten by **predators**, such as birds. If the weather is too wet, cold, or windy, they cannot fly. Some do not survive.

When they finally arrive in Mexico, the butterflies rest on fir trees for the winter. Millions of monarch butterflies cover the trees in a blanket of orange.

Monarch butterflies only live for a few months. Those that migrate have never made the journey before. No one knows for sure how they find their way.

In the spring, monarch butterflies fly the long journey north again. Once they have laid their eggs, the butterflies die.

129

Building Bugs

Some creepy-crawlies are capable of making incredible structures! Termites are tiny **insects** that live in large **colonies**. Together, they create towering nests that change the landscape.

Chimney

Eggs and young

Queen

Termite colonies are made up of one queen and many workers. As well as looking after the queen, eggs, and babies, the workers build the nest.

Workers mix soil with spit and poop to build mounds. Gradually, the mounds get bigger, harder, and taller. Some termite mounds are 5 m (17 ft) tall!

The Darwin's bark spider from Madagascar spins the largest web of any spider. Its web can stretch across a river, trapping insects in superstrong silk.

Weaver ants build their nests in trees. The ants push leaves together, weaving the edges with silk made by their **larvae**.

Inside the mound is a network of corridors and chambers for the queen and the young. A chimney runs through the middle, bringing fresh air inside.

Queen

Workers

The huge queen termite never leaves the mound. She can grow to be the length of a human finger—100 times bigger than a worker!

The caddisfly larva lives underwater. For protection, it builds a case around itself. It spins together sand, shells, twigs, and leaves with a silk it makes.

131

Slithering Along

If you go for a walk after a rain shower, you may see slugs, snails, and worms slithering about. These soft-bodied invertebrates must keep their skin damp in order to survive.

A snail has a shell on its back and hides inside when in danger. The shell grows with the snail, so it always fits perfectly.

Eye stalks

Slugs and snails move along on a muscular "foot." Their eyes are on the end of long stalks. Two feelers taste the air and ground in front.

Slugs and snails have tongues covered with thousands of tiny teeth. They eat plants, scraping and filing them with their toothy tongues.

Slime is very important for slugs and snails. It helps them slide along, stick to surfaces, and keeps their bodies from drying out.

Slime trail

Feelers

Earthworms eat rotting leaves and dead plants, recycling them into soil. They also mix air and water into soil, helping plants grow.

Make a Bug Hotel

Get up close to creepy-crawlies, and make a mini bug hotel for your backyard. You'll need a clean, empty drink carton, some kitchen or toilet paper tubes, and lots of natural materials.

1

Ask an adult to help you cut out a rectangle from one side of your carton, leaving 2 cm (1 in) around the edges.

2

Cut some pieces of cardboard tubes, so that they fit into the carton with the holes facing outward. Fill the carton with the tubes.

3

When the carton is tightly packed with tubes, add your natural materials. Try using twigs, bark, dry leaves, moss, grass, and stones.

4

Find a sheltered place for your bug hotel—perhaps by a fence or under a bush. Check every day to see if any bug buddies have checked in!

Why not paint or decorate your bug hotel?

Cunning Predators

Not all bugs are happy to chomp through plants and leaves—some prefer a meatier meal. Assassin bugs are creepy-crawly killers with very unusual hunting habits.

Assassin bugs are the fierce **predators** of the **insect** world, which is how they get their name. They often hunt by sneaking up on their **prey**.

The trapdoor spider's burrow has a hinged lid made from silk and soil. When it senses prey, the spider bursts through the trapdoor and attacks.

The assassin bug stabs and injects saliva (spit) into prey using its sharp mouthparts. The prey's insides turn to liquid, which the assassin sucks up.

After it has eaten, a young ant-eating assassin bug piles empty ant bodies on its back. It can carry 20 ants at a time!

The ants are held with sticky threads that the bug makes on its back. It's believed that this strange disguise puts off would-be attackers.

The Amazonian giant centipede hunts in caves by hanging from the ceiling. It will catch a bat as it flies, killing it with its venomous fangs.

137

Swarm of Locusts

When animals gather together in huge numbers, it is called a swarm. A locust is the name for a type of grasshopper that swarms with devastating effects.

Locusts are **insects** with strong back legs, making them great at jumping. They rub their legs on their wings to create a loud chirping noise.

Locusts spend most of the time alone. However, changes in the weather and a lack of food can make locusts look and behave differently.

The locusts gather together, forming a large swarm of millions of insects. The swarm flies huge distances for days or weeks at a time.

When the swarm lands, the locusts eat any plants they find. The hungry insects can completely strip and destroy farmers' crops.

Midges are tiny flies that swarm in order to find a **mate**. They form shimmering, cloud-like swarms in the early evening, often near water.

Why We Need Bugs

Although some can bite or sting, and others can eat our plants, **insects** and creepy-crawlies are an important part of nature. We cannot live without them!

Many animals, such as birds, small mammals, and reptiles, depend on insects and other bugs for their food.

Insects are a great source of food for people, too. In some cultures, bugs are considered a delicious snack. We also farm bees for the sweet honey they make.

Some insects, such as butterflies, bees, and moths are pollinators. This means that they help plants grow new ones by spreading their **pollen** from flower to flower.

Insects can help us by eating bugs that harm our crops and gardens.

Invertebrates such as worms and beetles help break down dead plants, recycling **nutrients** back into the soil.

Insects Quiz

Put your knowledge about insects to the test. Decide if these sentences are true or false, then check your answers on page 191. No peeping!

1 Flies can only fly in one direction.

2 There are around 40,000 different types of beetle.

3 Tarantulas live in huge webs.

4 Monarch butterflies can only fly in good weather.

5 Slugs and snails have toothy tongues.

6 Locusts are really quiet creatures.

All About Trees

Tremendous Trees

Every animal on Earth needs trees ... and that includes you! Trees give us an important gas called oxygen. All animals and people need to breathe oxygen in order to live.

Trees provide homes and shelter for millions of different plants and animals. Wood from trees can be used to make buildings, furniture, and paper.

Trees produce food for animals and people, such as **seeds**, nuts, and fruit. Some creatures, such as insects, feed on the bark and leaves of trees.

Burning fossil fuels produces gases such as **carbon dioxide**. Trees convert this gas into oxygen. Too much carbon dioxide makes the world hotter, so trees help keep our planet a comfortable temperature for everything that lives here.

Large areas filled with trees are called forests and woodlands. They are important **habitats** (homes) for many different kinds of plants and animals.

145

Broadleaf Trees

There are lots of different types of trees. Broadleaf trees have lots of leaves that they lose in winter. They are also called **deciduous** trees. Deciduous trees grow in many parts of the world.

A broadleaf tree has leaves that are wide and flat in shape. Oak, maple, and beech are common types of broadleaf trees.

Horse chestnut leaf

Crown

The very top of a tree is called the crown. A broadleaf tree usually has a wide, bushy crown. Each type of tree has its own shape.

The branches of a broadleaf tree grow outward, away from the trunk. Its branches are often crooked. As it grows, the tree gets wider and taller.

Horse chestnut tree

Broadleaf trees grow flowers called blossoms. The flowers produce fruits and **seeds**. Birds and animals like to eat the seeds and fruit.

Blossoms

147

Wonderful Woodland

A woodland **habitat** is green and shady. In a deciduous woodland, the trees, plants, and even some animals change along with the seasons. Lots of plants and animals live among the trees.

Birch

Hazel

Woodpecker

Many woodland animals feed on the nuts, **seeds**, and berries from the trees. Some woodland creatures hibernate (sleep) during the cold winter months.

Sycamore

Oak

Bluebells

The trees give shelter and protection to many different plants and animals. Squirrels will scurry up a tree trunk to escape danger.

Plants that live here are able to live in the cool shade of the wood. In spring, a beautiful carpet of bluebells can be seen in some woodlands.

149

The Life of a Tree

Some trees can live for thousands of years. But even the oldest trees started as a small **seed**. Trees need warmth and light from the sun, and water from rain, to grow strong and healthy.

2

The seed sprouts a shoot, which pushes up through the surface of the soil. The tiny shoot is called a seedling.

1

Root

This seed is an acorn. It falls from the tree as the weather gets colder. Then, in the spring, the first root breaks through the outer layer of the acorn. This is called **germination**.

As the seedling grows taller and stronger, it begins to look like a small tree.

3

4

After many years, the tree becomes a "mature" oak tree. It can now flower and make acorns of its own.

5

Beetle

Fungus

An oak tree can live for hundreds of years. When it dies and rots, it becomes an important **habitat** and source of food for wildlife.

Lovely Leaves

A tree's leaves do an important job. They make food for the tree using sunlight, water, and air. This process is called photosynthesis.

Carbon dioxide from the air goes in through tiny holes in the underside of the leaf.

Stem

The tree's roots take in water from the ground. The water travels to the leaf through the stem and veins.

Leaves take in energy from the sunlight. The leaves are flat and wide to take in as much sunlight as they can.

Vein

The leaves turn the carbon dioxide and water into **oxygen** and a type of sugar called **glucose**.

The tree uses the glucose to grow. The veins carry glucose to rest of the tree. The leaves release oxygen into the air.

Leaf Rubbing

Leaves come in all shapes and sizes. Next time you go for a walk outdoors, collect some different types of leaves. Then use them to create a beautiful artwork!

Place your leaves on a sheet of paper. Arrange them however you like. You could create a scene or make a pattern.

A "simple leaf" has one segment, or blade, which is attached to a stem.

Beech

Cover the leaves with another piece of paper the same size. Holding the paper in place, carefully rub over each leaf with a crayon.

Keep rubbing over each leaf until your picture is finished. You don't need to stick to green crayons—try using blue, purple, or even create rainbow stripes!

A "compound leaf" is made up of lots of leaf-shaped leaflets connected to a stemlike middle part.

Can you spot the veins and stem in your leaf rubbings?

Are your leaves simple or compound?

Black walnut

Animal Homes

Many different creatures build their homes in and around trees. The trees can be a safe place to hide from predators. Trees also provide strong and sturdy building materials.

Beavers live in rivers near woodland. They cut down trees with their powerful teeth, and use the wood to build dams. The dams make pools where the beavers build their homes, called "lodges."

Drey

Lodge

Squirrels build nests called dreys in the hollows and branches of trees. They build a drey using twigs and leaves, then line it with moss and feathers to make it snug.

Hornets are a large type of wasp. Hornets live in groups called colonies. Their paper-like nests can be found in hollow trees. Hornet nests are made from chewed-up wood.

Tawny owls make their nests in holes in **deciduous** trees, such as oaks. They sleep during the day. At night, tawny owls hunt for mice and voles.

Dam

Amazing Rain Forest

A rain forest is warm and wet all year round. The Amazon Rain Forest in South America is the largest rain forest in the world. A rain forest has different "layers," where many types of plants and animals live.

The top of the trees is called the canopy. Monkeys swing from branch to branch, while bright birds fly through the canopy.

Cacao tree

Rubber tree

The bottom part of the rain forest is the forest floor. There isn't much sunlight, so not many plants grow here. Creatures feed on leaves that have fallen from above.

Only the tallest trees, such as Brazil-nut trees, grow through the top of the canopy. This part of the forest is called the "emergent layer."

The "undergrowth" is the layer below the canopy. Bushes and smaller trees grow here. Many trees have enormous leaves, so they can catch as much sunlight as possible.

Brazil-nut tree

← Palm tree

Leafcutter ants

Strong and Sturdy

As a tree grows, it gets taller and wider. It produces new branches, which give the tree its shape. The thick trunk and tough bark give a tree its strength.

The bark is like the tree's skin. It helps to protect the tree from damage by animals. It also stops it from being harmed by very hot or cold weather.

Rings

The tree trunk makes a new ring each year, as it grows upward and outward. You can tell how old a tree is by counting the rings.

Smooth bark

The bark near the base of the tree can be cracked and rough. As you look further up the tree, the bark gets smoother.

Rough bark

The trunk is wider at the base. The trunk is strong so that it can support the branches above. The distance around the trunk is called the girth.

Four Seasons

Broadleaf trees can look very different, depending on the time of year. Follow this red maple tree as it changes from season to season.

1

In spring, buds appear on the bare branches. As the days become longer and warmer, tiny flowers grow on the tree and green leaves grow.

Flowers

4

The leaves fall from the red maple tree. During the cold winter months, the branches stay bare—ready for it to begin all over again!

2

During the warm summer months, the tree is covered thickly with glossy, green leaves. The tree produces a "winged" fruit, which contains **seeds**.

Seeds

3

As the weather gets colder and there is less sunlight, the leaves start to change. They turn yellow, then orange, and finally bright red.

Making Seeds

New plants and trees grow from **seeds**. To make seeds, a plant needs **pollen** from another plant of the same type. This means pollen needs to move around.

Pollen

Many plants and trees use animals to spread their pollen. When bees collect **nectar** from a flower, they get covered in sticky pollen, which they then carry to other flowers.

164

When the plant has what it needs, it makes seeds. When the seeds have grown, they need to move to where they can grow. Many trees grow fruit around their seeds. The seeds are planted when an animal eats a piece of fruit and then poops out the seeds!

Spiky seeds called burrs can hitch a ride to a new spot by sticking to the fur of a passing animal.

Burrs

Some seeds float in the air. Next time you see a dandelion plant, blow on it and watch the seeds fly away.

Evergreen Trees

We call some trees "evergreen" because they stay green all year round. Unlike **broadleaf** trees, evergreens do not lose their leaves in winter. Evergreen trees can be found all over the world.

Evergreen leaves have a tough, waxy surface, which helps them hold onto water. The leaves can be shaped like needles, or like scales.

Douglas fir tree needle

Cone

Conifers are a type of evergreen tree. They do not have flowers or fruit. Instead, they produce cones which carry the tree's **seeds**. The cones have a scaly surface.

Conifers have tall, straight trunks, with regularly spaced branches. A conifer has an even shape, looking the same on both sides.

The wood from evergreen trees is very strong and is often used for buildings and furniture. Some conifers, such as pine and cypress trees, have a nice smell.

Coniferous Forest

A coniferous forest is a place that is filled with conifers. Coniferous forests are often found in cooler parts of the world.

← Pine

Many conifers have special features to help them live in the cold. They have long, sharp needles. The needles allow snow to slide off them easily.

Nuthatch

Moose

Fir

Spruce

The trees of a
coniferous forest
include pines, firs,
and spruces. They
grow tall and straight
and have a similar
shape to each other.

Wolf

The animals that live in coniferous
forests also have clever ways to
cope with cold weather. Wolves
have thick fur to keep them warm.

Beautiful Blossoms

Some trees put on a beautiful show in the springtime. Their branches are covered with pretty, sweet-smelling flowers called blossoms.

Japanese cherry blossom trees produce bright pink flowers. The blossoms usually only last for around a week before the petals float to the ground.

Inside each flower is a kind of sweet juice called **nectar** and a sticky powder called **pollen**. In order for the tree to make **seeds**, pollen needs to be spread to other trees.

The blossoms smell nice in order to attract insects, such as bees and butterflies. These creatures drink the nectar from the flowers and collect pollen on their bodies.

Once the blossoms on the tree have died away, the tree will go on to make fruit and seeds.

171

Extreme Trees

The tallest trees on Earth are Californian redwoods. These evergreen trees grow along the West Coast of the United States.

Redwoods can grow more than 100 m (330 ft) tall—that's taller than the Statue of Liberty! The base of the trunks can be 9 m (30 ft) wide.

They have somewhat shallow roots compared to their great height. This means that the trees sway in the wind. Occasionally, they fall over.

It takes hundreds of years for a redwood to become fully grown. They can live for up to 2,000 years.

Although the redwood is the tallest, some trees can be wider. The widest tree in the world is thought to be a cypress tree in Mexico. Its trunk is more than 11 m (36 ft) wide.

Out in the Open

Trees that live on the grasslands of Africa have to be tough, because there is so little rain. They have special ways of holding onto water.

Acacia

The tough acacia tree has long roots that seek out water deep underground. Its long, sharp thorns protect the tree from being eaten by browsing animals.

Giraffe

Sociable weaver bird

Acacia thorn

174

Trees are important for wildlife. Elephants and giraffes eat their leaves. They also provide shelter from the burning sun.

Baobab

The baobab tree has an enormous trunk. It uses the trunk to store water. The baobab's thick bark does not burn easily, which helps protect it from fires.

175

Fantastic Fruit

After the blossoms fall away, flowering trees will start to grow fruits. A fruit is the part of the tree that contains its **seeds**.

Early in summer, tiny fruits begin to appear on apple trees. They grow bigger and bigger throughout the warm summer months.

Badger

Fieldfare

Fruit attracts wildlife. Birds like to peck at fallen apples. Fruit also makes a tasty meal for badgers and mice.

Core

Seeds

By the end of the summer, the apples are ripe. If they are not picked by people, they fall from the tree onto the ground below.

Codling caterpillar

The caterpillars of codling moths make a tiny hole in some apples and eat their way to the middle. The middle of the apple is called the core. Apple seeds are in the core.

177

Taking Root

The roots are the parts of the tree that are usually underground. They are the first part of the tree to grow. Trees depend on their roots to live.

The roots of a tree spread very wide. Some are often just under the surface. Sometimes, you can see roots that have broken through the ground.

Surface root

The first root, called the taproot, grows straight down under the tree. This helps to hold the tree firmly to the ground. Other roots grow in different directions.

Taproot

Some trees have roots that grow deep into the ground, while others have shallow roots. Most conifers have very shallow roots.

The tips of the roots take in water and **nutrients** from the soil. The water travels through the roots to the rest of the tree.

Plant a Seed

Even the tallest tree was once just a small seed. Plant sunflower, pea, or bean seeds, and watch them grow. You'll also need a glass jar, some paper towels, water, and time!

1

Pour a little water into a glass jar, and swill it around so the sides get wet. Push paper towels inside the jar.

2

Sprinkle a little water onto the seeds, and place them between the paper and the side of the jar. The damp paper should hold the seeds in place.

Bean seed

Root

3 Sprinkle water in the jar every day or so, to keep the paper from drying out. The seeds will start to swell. After a few days, the seed will split and the first root will appear.

4 Next, the stem will sprout upward. Once the seedling has leaves, it can make its own food. Plant your seedling in a pot of soil, and see how big it gets!

Stem

Roots

In order to germinate (develop), seeds need water, air, and the right temperature. Trees take years to grow. Many tree seeds need the cold of at least one winter before they can germinate.

Tropical Trees

Palm trees are able to live in places that are very warm. They grow in **rain forests**, deserts, and on the edges of **tropical** beaches.

Palms do not have branches. Instead, they have lots of large leaves that grow out of the top of the tree.

The tough, leathery leaves are known as "fronds." They are pointed at the tips, so that water falls off them easily in a tropical rainstorm.

A palm tree trunk is tall and fairly straight, and about the same thickness all the way up. The trunk is able to bend in tropical winds and storms.

The roots of palm trees stretch deep underground to find water. They do not grow as thick as other types of tree roots.

Trees in Danger

One-third of the land on Earth is covered
with forests, but this is changing.
People cut down trees to make
space for farmland and new towns.
This harms the **environment**.

In a natural forest,
hundreds of different
types of trees and plants
grow. The animals that
live there depend on this
variety of plant life. This
is called **biodiversity**.

When forests are cleared,
many trees and plants die.
The animals that lived there
lose their homes.

Farms often grow just
a few different types
of plants, which means
that fewer animals can
live there.

People also make lots of waste called **pollution**, which can harm trees, plants, and animals.

Sometimes, fires start in forests. They can start by themselves in hot, dry weather. They can also be started by people. Forest fires can destroy hundreds of trees.

How to Help

Trees help our planet to be healthy. They clean our air and provide homes for many different types of animals. Find out how you can help protect our precious trees.

Try to use less paper. Make sure you write or draw on both sides of a sheet of paper, and use handkerchiefs, rather than tissues. These are great ways to use less.

When you really cannot use card and paper again, put it in the recycling box. This means that your waste paper is processed, so that it can be used to make new things.

Help create a clean living **environment** for trees by picking up litter whenever you can. Not only does litter look unpleasant, it can also pollute the soil and water needed for trees to grow.

Planting a tree is a great way to do something good for the environment. Many organizations hold tree-planting days. If you have outdoor space, you could plant your own tree.

Trees Quiz

Put your knowledge about trees to the test. Decide if these sentences are true or false, then check your answers on page 191. No peeping!

1 The top of a tree is called the crown.

2 An acorn grows into a maple tree.

3 Hornet nests are made from chewed-up wood.

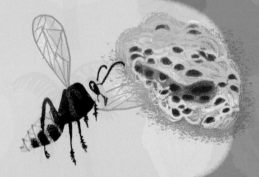

4 You can tell a tree's age by counting its rings.

5 Evergreen trees lose their leaves in winter.

6 Japanese cherry blossoms are in flower for months.

Glossary

Abdomen   The rear part of an insect's or spider's body.

Amphibians   A group of animals that can live in water and on land, such as frogs, toads, and salamanders.

Antennae   An invertebrate's feelers, used for sensing.

Arachnid   An arthropod with eight legs, such as a spider, scorpion, or mite.

Arthropod   An invertebrate with jointed legs, exoskeleton, and a body divided into segments.

Birds of prey   A group of birds that hunt animals using their claws.

Biodiversity   The variety of plants and animals found in a particular area.

Broadleaf   A type of deciduous tree, with a bushy shape and wide, flat leaves.

Canopy   The top layer of trees in a forest.

Carbon dioxide   A gas found in the air. Plants take in carbon dioxide, and animals breathe it out.

Carnivore   An animal that only eats meat.

Colony   A group of animals that live together.

Compound eye   An eye that is made up of many tiny lenses, rather than just one.

Coniferous   Mostly evergreen trees that produce cones.

Coral reef   A large underwater structure made up of lots of hard coral joined together.

Crest   A natural growth on the head of an animal.

Crustacean   A type of arthropod such as a crab, or lobster. Most crustaceans live in the sea, but woodlice live on land.

Deciduous   Describes trees or shrubs that lose their leaves seasonally.

Environment   The surroundings of an area, including living things and non-living things.

Endangered   A living thing that is in danger of dying out.

Evergreen   A tree or shrub that keeps its leaves and remains green throughout the year.

Exoskeleton   A hard outer skeleton.

Fledgling   A young bird that is ready to fly and leave the nest.

Flightless bird   A bird that is naturally unable to fly, such as a penguin or an ostrich.

Flock   A group of animals.

Germination   The development of a seed into a plant.

Gill   The paired body part of a fish and some amphibians that allows them to take in oxygen from water.

Glucose   A type of sugar.

Habitat The natural home of an animal or plant.

Herbivore An animal that only eats plants.

Herd A large group of animals that feed on grass or other plants.

Insect An arthropod with six legs and three body parts.

Invertebrate An animal that has no bony skeleton inside its body.

Larvae Insects or other creatures in their very young form.

Life cycle The growth and life of a living thing from birth to death.

Mammal A type of animal that has hair and drinks its mother's milk.

Marine mammal A mammal that lives some or all of its life in the sea.

Marsupials A group of mammals that look after their babies in a pouch on their belly.

Mate An animal's partner for breeding.

Metamorphosis The process of an animal changing from one form to another as it grows into an adult.

Migration A seasonal journey that an animal makes, in order to feed, breed, or escape the cold.

Murmuration A gathering of a large group of birds, usually starlings, that fly and change direction together.

Nectar A sweet liquid produced by flowers, that animals like to eat.

Nocturnal Active at night.

Nutrients Substances that are important for the growth and development of plants and animals.

Nutritious Contains nutrients.

Nymph The early stage of some animals' lives before they grow into their adult form.

Oxygen A natural gas in the air that is necessary for all life on Earth.

Photosynthesis The process by which plants and trees make their own food using sunlight, water, and carbon dioxide.

Plankton Tiny living things, including plants and animals, that float in fresh or seawater.

Poisonous Contains substances that are harmful when touched or eaten.

Pollen A sticky powder that plants produce in order to make more plants.

Pollution Harmful waste, including rubbish and chemicals, that dirties the air, land, or sea.

Predator An animal that hunts and eats other animals.

Prey An animal that is hunted and eaten by other animals.

Proboscis A tube-like mouthpart used by some insects to suck up liquids.

Pupa A stage in the life cycle of some insects when they change from a larva into an adult.

Rain forest A thick forest found in warm, wet areas of the world.

Reptile A scaly creature that lays eggs and must warm itself in the sun.

Roost To settle down to rest, or sleep.

Seed The part of a plant that grows into a new plant.

Talons The claws of a bird of prey.

Thorax The middle part of an insect's body.

Tropical Characteristic of an area of the world that is warm or hot all year round.

Venom Harmful substances injected into another animal by biting or stinging.

Venomous Contains venom.

Answers

Animals Quiz

1 False—elephants live in large family groups.
2 True.
3 True.
4 False—porcupine fish are poisonous.
5 True.
6 False—dolphins are marine mammals.

Birds Quiz

1 False—Andean condors feed on the bodies of large dead animals.
2 False—tailorbirds "sew" leaves together to make their nests.
3 True.
4 False—herring gulls will eat almost anything they can find!
5 True.
6 True.

Insects Quiz

1 False—flies can fly forward, backward, and hover.
2 True.
3 False—tarantulas hide in silk-lined burrows.
4 True.
5 True.
6 False—locusts make a very loud chirping noise.

Trees Quiz

1 True.
2 False—an acorn grows into an oak tree.
3 True.
4 True.
5 False—evergreen trees keep their leaves all year round.
6 False—the blossoms only last for about a week.

Index